Raw Family

A True Story of Awakening

Victoria, Igor, Sergei and Valya Boutenko

Raw Family Publishing

Raw Family Publishing
P.O. Box 172
Ashland, OR 97520, U.S.A.

www.RawFamily.com

Library of Congress Catalog Card Number 00-108696
ISBN-13: 978-0-9704-8195-5
ISBN-10: 0-9704819-5-0
Printed in Canada on 100% post-consumer recycled paper

DISCLAIMER: The information contained in this book is
not intended as medical advice. The Boutenkos do not
recommend cooked foods or standard medical practices.
The authors, publishers and/or distributors will not assume
responsibility for any adverse consequences resulting from
adopting the lifestyle described herein.

Dedication

*We dedicate this book to people who are
helping others by being a good example.*

Acknowledgements

We thank all the people in the world who speak the truth.

We thank all our dear friends throughout the world who inspired us to present thinking.

We thank all Editors, Financiers, Readers, Artists and Printers for their kindness and patience.

Special thanks to Elizabeth Bechtold for financing our book.

Contents

Fable

I was riding in a comfortable bus with many friends. Outside the weather was stormy with pouring rain, lightning and wind were bending trees to the ground. In the bus was pleasant music, laughter, good company and relaxing seats. The aroma of mounds of shrimp was everywhere and we were ready to eat!

While looking through the window I suddenly saw a sign very clearly. It said, "No gas services next 500 miles"! Automatically I looked over the driver's shoulder and noticed that the gas gauge was close to the red mark. I told him about the sign, and he retorted, "It couldn't be! You must've been mistaken. I think there will be one soon." As it was, the driver was not pleased with my interrupting the joke he was telling.

I remembered very clearly what I saw and thought that surely someone else in the bus must have seen it. I went through the bus and asked my friends. Nobody saw the sign and, what was more surprising, nobody cared!

I began to realize that we'd have to walk back many miles as the bus was quickly taking us farther and farther toward the point of no return. I knew it was important to turn our bus back, but my friends began to feel irritated. I grabbed my backpack and asked the driver to let me out. Some of my friends started to tell me, "Hey, you'll get all wet and cold. Wait for the shrimp first. Don't leave us. Don't you like our company?"

Ignoring them, I jumped off the bus at the first opportunity. But it wasn't long before I was very cold and scared. For a while, I doubted my own wisdom. How nice it was in a warm bus . . .

I started to walk faster to get warmer. Walking in wet shoes soon gave me bad blisters. There were more busses filled with people and music following the route my bus had taken. I couldn't believe that I was the only one who saw the sign.

It took me two hours to reach the sign. I read it again. I was glad that it was real and I felt sorry for my friends. But I had done my best to let them know. I continued walking. I fell into some kind of numbness or meditation and didn't notice how it started to light up in the eastern sky.

Suddenly I saw a barefoot man standing on the road. Smiling, he asked, "Did you get off the bus? Me too. I'm so glad to see you. I've been walking alone for fourteen days already. You are the first one I've seen since then."

I was surprised that he didn't look tired or depressed. In fact, he looked happy and refreshed. I told him about my blisters, and how I was tired and hungry. Instead of sympathy, the man began to tell me his story. He said that he had begun to really enjoy walking. He said, *everybody would have to get off the bus.*

Going Down

Victoria: We came to the United States from Russia in 1989 when I was invited by the Community College of Denver to teach students about Russian president Gorbachev and *Perestroika*. At first, the cultural shock was great. I remember we felt inspired and hopeless at the same time. When I saw signs on the street benches that read, "Rent a bench!" I wrote to my mother, "Life here is very expensive. Even to sleep on a bench people have to pay rent."

On our arrival from Russia, I was not very fat. I was 180 pounds, a "normal" Russian woman. When I visited my very first American supermarket and saw all those multi-colored boxes, I told my husband that I wanted to try them all! And I think I did. In two short years, I gained 100 pounds.

From that day in the first supermarket, I noticed that many foods in the boxes were not as tasty as I had expected. While still in Russia, I saw "Dunkin Donuts" in so many movies that I was anxious to try them. When I tried one, I could not understand why in the world anyone would like Dunkin Donuts. I had to try them three times to become completely addicted. Then I began to wonder why I didn't like them before.

Then things got even worse. We had opened six very successful businesses, become rich, bought a big house and slept on a huge, fancy, very soft bed. We went out every night to every fancy or exotic restaurant in Denver and the suburbs.

From that kind of "full" life (I'd rather say fool life), I developed serious health problems. My left arm numbed every night. My veins were popping out. I developed persistent arrhythmia, which is an unsteady heart beat. At the same time, my father in Russia had his second heart attack. When I talked with him on the phone, he described his symptoms. They matched mine so closely that from that moment I never knew if I would awaken the next morning.

My doctor told me that I had to lose weight. I signed up for a life membership at a health club but never seemed to find time to go there again. I subscribed to *Weight Watchers* magazine and had wonderful fantasies while reading it. Then I went to the *Slim-Fast* workshop. Soon I signed up for another popular weight-loss program. I got an itchy rash from eating their special food, but I didn't lose a single ounce.

As a result of all these failures and wishful thinking, I began to fall into a deep depression.

Soon I was doubting the very reason for continuing to live. I considered my life finished and any changes seemed impossible. I gave up. I was going down.

Valya: I knew about my mother's terrible heart condition and my father's arthritis. I also knew that I had asthma, but I thought asthma was normal, just fine.

Sergei: I remember the past. My mother was always so tired. She never took us places. Instead, she'd hire somebody to take us to a movie, or to the park.

My sister and I were bored and were constantly chewing something. I started to gain weight. All summer long I would sit on our expensive Lazy Boy couch and think of a good activity with which to entertain myself.

We had constant mood swings (especially me) and one moment I'd crush some toys or old machinery with rocks or a hammer. The next minute I would be too tired and lazy to walk from the couch to the door to let my dog out.

When I was about 9 years old, I started noticing disturbing changes in my health. After I gorged myself one Halloween on a pillowcase of candy, my mother found me unconscious on the bathroom floor.

My mom rushed me to the doctor, who told us that I had incurable juvenile diabetes, and that I had to go on insulin immediately. He said I would have to give myself shots for the rest of my life and there was nothing more he could do. My mom and I were shocked. Mother decided to go home and "think about it."

As we were leaving the doctor's office, rivers of tears poured from mom's eyes. She cried all that night, and when I was leaving for school she was still sitting in the kitchen with tears in her eyes.

Valya: One day I came home from school and found my mom in tears. I learned that Sergei had juvenile diabetes. "What's that?" I asked. She told me it was an incurable disease which would cause him to lose his eyesight, and kidneys. Later he wouldn't be able to use his legs and he'd possibly die in a coma. He would have to give himself shots daily. After this conversation, I had thoughts that Sergei might die! My brother, die!

Victoria: When I learned about Sergei's diabetes, it awoke in me my mother's instinct, which appeared to be stronger than my depression and disease. It saved his life, and mine too. When I heard the diagnosis "juvenile diabetes," I was so shocked and horrified that I lost my appetite for a couple of days. I remember thinking, "God! Why is this happening to my son?" That filled me with self-pity and increased my suffering. Deep inside I felt very strongly that to put Sergei on insulin would be completely wrong. I decided to do some research.

Since I had studied to be a medical nurse years ago in Russia, I decided to buy medical books. I read that blindness and kidney failure could occur as a result of using insulin, not from diabetes itself. Throughout all of these books there were many statements that there is not even the slightest chance of cure for this type of diabetes. For example, the *American Diabetes Association Complete Guide to Diabetes* said: "The only way to treat Type 1 diabetes is to give the body another source of insulin. Usually, this is done through injections of insulin. However, new experimental approaches also show some promise. Patients with Type 1 diabetes have experienced miraculous results from pancreas transplants." Reading these medical books only strengthened my decision not to put Sergei on insulin. We bought him a blood monitor, and he began checking his blood sugar several times a day.

I took Sergei off white sugar and white flour. However, this didn't make any difference in his blood tests. I didn't know what to do next. In the bookstore there was a sea of information, all of which was contradictory. I didn't have much time; the doctor threatened to report me to social services because I wouldn't put Sergei on insulin. I decided that I needed only the information that worked. I wanted to know how people become healthy.

That's when I started to notice how different people look. I saw that some people look much healthier than others. One day I overcame my embarrassment and began asking healthy-looking people what they knew about alternative treatments for diabetes.

Then one day at my bank, I got in line behind a

radiant and happy woman. I asked her my question and she smiled. "Of course, the body can heal everything. I healed my colon cancer fifteen years ago." I invited her to lunch. Elisabeth smiled again: "I cannot eat your lunch, but we can talk." What Elisabeth said was shocking (what do you mean, everything raw?). At the same time I had a very confident feeling inside myself.

Elisabeth answered all my questions, and gave me an old book about raw food. No matter how scary everything sounded, it made sense. My heart told me it was right.

Elisabeth, wherever you are, little shy lady, thank you!

To Be Raw, or Not to Be Raw?

Victoria: I went to the bookstore and found books on raw foods. I enjoyed reading them! These books had more in them; more than just health information. The authors seemed to be free and happy people. I wanted to be free and happy too.

Sergei: Mom was reading day and night, surviving on only a few hours sleep each night. I remember noticing a growing smile on her face during those days.

Victoria: *In the morning, while holding on tight to my heavy cup of strong coffee and digging my teeth into a warm bagel with my favorite cream cheese, I was trying to imagine having a raw breakfast. I asked myself, When should we start eating raw food? And how? "Tomorrow I will start." But the next morning I had my coffee in my hands before I was even able to think. I looked at my husband who was enjoying his morning feast consisting of three bagels, two muffins, and a beer mug of coffee. I sighed.*

It was Christmas time and almost two months since Sergei had been diagnosed with diabetes. The poor child had difficulty sleeping every night, he had circles around his eyes and his blood sugar was high. His grades at school went below average.

I was anxious to try raw foods, but couldn't imagine doing it on my own. I tried to talk to Igor. He said: "If it was this easy, all the doctors would recommend it. But they don't. And they are well-educated people. You can try it, but you see, food unites people. If you will eat that crazy diet, eventually it will separate us." I didn't know what to say, except that we had to do something.

Igor's Story

I **gor:** I was skeptical, because I had tried a "healthy" diet before, and it was a very negative experience for me.

Many years ago in Russia, when I was 20, I became a member of a large vegetarian group. All their healthy food was so bland and so lean. I craved the food that I grew up with: our traditional aromatic Russian borscht with pork, fragrant rice pilaf with lamb and a good piece of a chocolate cake for dessert. Nevertheless, I was able to stay on a vegetarian diet for quite a long time because I had strong willpower.

But I became weak, my energy was very low, cavities formed in all my teeth, I lost lots of weight and my buttocks were drooping behind me. I put up with eating tasteless dishes during the day and was cheating in my dreams. I envied all those around me who were allowed to eat anything they wanted. Then my inner "wisdom" told me, "Why suffer? Why abide this? Are you happy? Forget about diets and enjoy life!" And I did.

Years passed. I became afraid of every new birthday, as I was aging rapidly. At 35 I was already accustomed to having shaky hands, bulging eyes, white hair, fatigue, and extreme irritability. I developed insomnia.

My arthritis was progressing rapidly, and the doctors told me that I would end up in a wheel-chair. On rainy days I had trouble tying my shoes.

I developed a very rapid pulse, and even when I was resting it was 150 beats per minute (normal is 60). At night, my wife couldn't put her head on my chest because, she said, my heart sounded as if it would blow up.

Finally, my pulse got so high that I couldn't work, and I went into the hospital. I was put on a bed, connected to the computer and had my pulse and blood pressure measured. My pulse was now 178. Five doctors gathered around me, discussing how to lower my pulse. They finally decided to pour six gallons of saline solution into my blood. After they did that my pulse went down five points, to 173.

Then the five doctors gathered in a circle around me again. Now they decided to stop my heart with an electric shock. They needed me to sign papers stating that I was aware that in 10 percent of the cases the heart will not start again. I refused and went home. I felt exhausted. In a few days we had a bill for $2,000 for "professional help."

Victoria: One day Igor woke up with a swollen neck. It looked like he had a tennis ball in his throat. He stood in front of the mirror touching his neck all morning. Igor was afraid that he had a cancerous tumor. I was afraid, too, but a sneaky thought passed through my mind: maybe now he'll go on raw food.

As soon as the children left for school, we left for the hospital. The doctor drew Igor's blood and announced that he had severe hyper-function of the thyroid. The doctor wanted to schedule a surgery soon to remove his thyroid. Igor then would need to take hormones for the rest of his life.

Igor was devastated. Having already endured nine surgeries for various ailments, (none of which made him any healthier), he refused the surgery. Now it was the doctor's turn to be devastated. He said that it was an incurable, degenerative, irreversible condition. "Look," he said, "here is the newest *Thyroid Sourcebook*. The doctor opened the book on his table, and I read: "Most people with thyroid disorder will simply get worse without treatment . . . after about fifteen years you would be a physical wreck."

Igor said, "I will go on a raw vegan diet." The doctor shook his head, "Actually, you're supposed to do just the opposite," and turned the page in the same book. I read where he was pointing: "When you're hyperthyroid . . . consume more butter, cream, cheese, and other dairy products . . . peanut butter, mayonnaise, and animal fat help as well . . . cut down on fruit juices and fresh fruits."

The doctor said, "Your disease is so far progressed. You'll have to come back."

On the way back home Igor was silent, but I knew what he was thinking.

Igor: *I was very sad. I didn't have any other choice than to go on a raw food diet. I thought, "What the heck! I will stay on a diet for two months and then will go back to what I like." This is exactly what I mentioned to my wife.*

When I came home several hours later, our kitchen was empty. "So that we don't have temptations," my wife explained.

The Beginning

Victoria: I went to the supermarket to buy raw food for my family. There I became amazed that from now on my shopping would be limited to the produce section. I didn't know what to buy, so I was going in circles around fruits and vegetables for a long time before I finished my shopping. Other people were still buying ham, cheese and coke. I was feeling so strange leaving the store without Popsicles for the children! It was one case when the mind said, "This is ridiculous! It cannot be true! You look funny!" But the heart whispered, "This is how everything works in life! If you don't do it now, you'll miss something forever. You'll regret it the rest of your life."

Valya: I will never forget this day. Sergei and I came home from school and I was plainly shocked. Most of the kitchen appliances were gone, but in their place was a huge new cutting board, which was strangely placed over the stove.

Sergei: I opened up the refrigerator and was horrified to see that there were no hotdogs, hamburgers, fish sticks or bread! Nothing to eat; only fruits and vegetables.

I told mom that I was willing to eat junk food and give myself shots but my mom said that she would rather die than allow that.

Valya: I wasn't really scared—until lunch time. We ate salad. For bread, we had slices of carrot. For dessert, we ate apples. Then I listened to my mother excitedly telling us that by eating apples and lettuce, we could cure our illness.

Sergei: I had never before heard of anyone who lived on fruit. I panicked. My mom calmed me down, pleading with me to try it for two weeks and see how I felt.

It's Really Happening!

Victoria: We went on raw food "cold turkey." The first day was the hardest. Truly, I was not sure if we would be able to stay on raw food until the end of the day. I had a terrible headache in the morning and throughout the day. I also felt weakness, fatigue, irritability, but worst of all was a constant appetite. In the evening my appetite grew into torturous hunger.

Valya was doing OK. Sergei had an immediate reaction.

Sergei: The first day on raw food was not easy for me. I got a terrible migraine headache. The pain was so intense that the school nurse sent me home. It was hard to deal with a headache when I couldn't take any Advil. I didn't eat anything. Mother bought me an enema bag, but I protested with disgust. The only thing that helped was sleep.

Next morning the headache was gone but now I had an earache. It was so violent that I stayed in bed. My father filled a bathtub with cold water. He told me to dip myself quickly in it every half hour. Doing this helped me a little bit.

Late in the afternoon my earache intensified again. I was lying in my bed crying. At night my

mother was lying next to me and gently massaging
my head, face and ears. As soon as I would begin to
feel better we both would fall asleep until the next
pain attack. Surprisingly, in the morning I felt
much better, and I was very hungry. I enjoyed my
breakfast, which consisted of pear/apple juice,
almonds and dates. I went to school, and mom
went to bed to get some sleep.

All that day I was in a very good mood. I felt
myself light and clear. At home I had a big salad
made with lettuce, tomatoes, cucumbers, onions, walnuts and olive oil. It tasted so good, that I changed
my mind about salads. Truly, I missed my "normal"
food, but I put up with it. So many shifts had already
happened, and it was only my third day on raw food.

Igor: My enthusiasm and my fear helped me to
get through the first morning and through the day.
But late in the evening I became shaky and angry.
I wanted to eat. I went to bed, but I couldn't sleep.
After rolling in bed for two or three hours I got up
and quietly tiptoed into the kitchen. I decided that
I would start raw food life tomorrow. I was going to
eat something like a baked potato or boiled egg, or
at least a piece of bread, whatever I could find. It
didn't take me very long to realize that in our now
empty kitchen there was nothing to make cooked
food with. Crunching my teeth I went back to bed
and kept rolling until finally I fell asleep.

In the morning, though, I didn't feel as tired as
usual. I enjoyed breakfast and lunch a lot. It was

delicious, but it didn't satisfy me. I wanted my "regular" food as desperately as people want a cigarette
when they quit smoking. I understood now how
addictive the cooked food is. In the evening everything happened again, only I was able to fall asleep a
little faster. I suffered like that for two long weeks.

Valya: I told myself I wasn't going to do this. My
parents never did anything for more than a couple of
days. So I cheated at school by eating "regular" foods.
I didn't want to go on raw food at all. I didn't even
want to try. None of my mom's raw foods tasted good
yet. I hardly liked apples, so I didn't want to do it.

But the excitement at home did not wear off.
Days passed, and then weeks.

Then one day at school in gym class we ran a
quarter of a mile. This really isn't far; sort of like
running around the soccer field one time. I finished
that race second to last. The very last girl walked.
It wasn't that my legs couldn't run fast, it was that
I couldn't breathe when I was running. It was my
asthma. There were some nights I could not
breathe at all, but I was sleeping and didn't notice.
But my parents were really worried and talked
about it in the morning. Then I thought, wow,
maybe I should go on raw food.

I noticed how my mother and father had both
lost weight. Not only did they look better, but they
were gentler and had more energy. So, I decided
that I would try it. I stopped cheating at school.

Soon we were running that quarter-mile again

at school. Now I could run much more easily. I
stopped breathing hard at night. I could move, I
could go to gymnastics, and I could run and do all
kinds of things I couldn't do before.

In the beginning at school it was pretty scary
for me what the kids would think of my lunch.
Usually, I brought a piece of onion and an avocado
and some of these really weird things that they
never had seen before. Other kids always bought
prepacked meals from the store. Here I was with
this little paper bag full of unusual things. They
asked, "What is that? Can I try some?" And I said,
"Sure, here, have a piece," and they would say,
"You know, this isn't bad, I could eat this."

One time I had a pomegranate. My friends loved
it so much, that there wasn't any left for me. I told
my mom that I needed two pomegranates next
time, one for me and one for other kids. Most of my
friends got interested in raw food, and I started to
enjoy my lunches a lot. Every time I brought something to lunch they were curious to know more, so
all the kids wanted to sit next to me.

Sergei: After two weeks, I noticed that my blood
sugar became more stable and I started feeling really
good.

I began to lose weight. I decided to stay on raw
food longer than two weeks.

Letting the Body Lead

Victoria: Soon we were to discover that our bodies have inner wisdom to lead us out of any wrongdoing.

After eating the same salad for two weeks everybody in my family got tired of it. I didn't know what to prepare and one day we "went out" to the salad bar at Wild Oats Health Store. There we noticed that everybody's plate was completely different. Igor had mostly sprouts; Sergei, cucumbers and tomatoes; Valya, radish and olives; and I, scallions and avocado. After lunch we all went to the fruit section and picked fruits for dessert. And again everybody picked different fruit: Igor, black grapes; Sergei, mango, or blueberries; Valya, figs; and I, persimmon.

We enjoyed eating at Wild Oats and went there very often. Soon it became obvious that every one of us had particular cravings.

When a couple of months later we met Dr. Bernard Jensen, a famous healer and teacher, he told us that Sergei needed to eat more mangoes and blueberries, because they provide important nutrients for healing the pancreas, and Valya needed to eat more figs and olives because they have healing properties for her asthma. We were very happy to hear that, because that was exactly what Sergei and Valya always wanted. That made us feel confident in our body wisdom.

Sergei: I remember how during the first month of living on raw food I had a "cucumber attack." I was looking through the refrigerator for something tasty, and out of the corner of my eye I saw it. It was beautiful, it was a cucumber. I bit into it and right away felt that this cucumber and I were destined for each other. I finished it quickly and realized that only one cucumber wasn't going to do it for me. I needed more to satisfy my craving.

My mom noticed that something strange was happening with me. She went to the store and bought two pounds of cucumbers. I ate those in one minute! Back to the store my mom went, only this time buying five pounds, not two. It wasn't long after she got home that I was on my last cuke.

This was the last straw for my mom. Running to the store time and time again wasn't exactly her favorite thing to do. She went back to the grocery store, this time buying me a whole case of cucumbers. When she stepped through the door of our house I was sitting on the couch awaiting her arrival impatiently. In no time I was in that case eating cucumbers! This time I ate only four more before my craving left me. The almost full case was going to have to find another way of getting used up, because I was over it.

100 Percent

Victoria: After about a month on raw food we really got bored with eating only salads. In one of the books I found information about CHI (Creative Health Institute) in Michigan. The book said that at this place they teach about raw food. We decided to drive to Michigan as soon as possible. It sounded unbelievable that we would meet other people resembling us.

Igor: At CHI we found ideal conditions for making raw a food diet most effective. Guests of CHI are completely isolated from any stress and temptations. The institute is located on the bank of the Cold Creek and surrounded by many beautiful trees.

We felt at home and among friends there. About twenty people from different states came to stay on a raw food diet for two weeks and to learn how to prepare tasty raw dishes. Every day we had different classes about the benefits of raw food. We learned how to make raw nut milks, seed cheese, raw soups, delicious dressings, live crackers and even cakes and pies!

Surprisingly to us, none of the staff were on a 100 percent raw food diet.

Victoria: In a certain way we were lucky, as we all got sick together and didn't have a choice. The addictive nature of cooked foods doesn't allow people to get off it slowly, similar to any other drug. One cannot usually stop drinking alcohol gradually. That's why there are AA meetings, where they urge newcomers to stop drinking altogether.

There is a big difference between drinking and eating cooked food. Everybody knows that drinking is bad, but the majority of people innocently believe that eating cooked food is not harmful, and is even necessary. That creates another difficulty for anyone who is trying to stay on a 100 percent raw diet.

I don't understand why many people think that it is easier to go on raw food gradually, slowly increasing the percentage of raw food in one's diet. Can we imagine somebody quitting drinking 50, 80 or 99 percent? "Yes, I quit drinking but I drink 1 percent of what I used to drink. One shot every other day." This is not being sober! Similarly, 99 percent raw is not raw. Some people argue with me: but you most likely consume little amounts of cooked foods accidentally, unknowingly. That's right. It's the same way sober people may eat a cake that has alcohol in its frosting, or dressing that has wine as one of ingredients. They will never even notice that. They are still sober. What is more important, they are not consuming alcohol *consciously*.

When you are 99 percent raw, this last 1 percent will keep the body calling for more addictive substance. It is very likely that at some meals you will consume 50 percent or even more of cooked food. On the other hand eliminating the last 1 percent makes the biggest difference. I've met very few people who were able to do it long enough. But that is when the real miracles begin to happen, when previously removed tonsils, teeth, appendixes and even gallbladders begin to regenerate.

Sergei: When I went on raw foods, I had eight fillings in my teeth. I remember that when mom was taking me to the dentist to fill cavities, those teeth were very tender. The doctor couldn't even touch them. After I had stayed on raw food for some months, the fillings started to pop out. I was surprised my teeth were not tender.

I went to my mom and said, "My teeth are rotting from this diet." She said, "Let's wait for a couple of weeks and see what happens."

Within several weeks, the darkness in my cavities began to whiten, and fill with enamel. At first, the enamel was yellowish, then it whitened, and then it hardened. Several months later, my teeth were as if they never had cavities. However, no one else in my family experienced dental regenerating as I did. I guess I'm just the lucky one. Now I have all my teeth completely restored. You may look into my mouth. But you cannot say which tooth ever had a cavity; they restored completely.

Valya: Before I went on raw food I had a big gap in front between my two front teeth and I couldn't whistle. They moved together within the first couple of months, which was really quick.

Victoria: By going 100 percent raw you are lowering your addiction to cooked foods to a very inactive, practically hibernation state. A cruel and destructive monster, Addiction to Cooked Food, turns into a soundly sleeping giant. Does this sleeping giant ever cease to exist? I don't think so. If you want him to continue to sleep, you must stay on raw food for the rest of your life, or all the miserable things will come back.

But while the giant is sleeping you can live!

Of course, to quit 100 percent is a shock to the body, but it is a positive shock. There are ways to soften that shock by other means without having to do it gradually. For this reason when we went on raw food we allowed ourselves any quantities and any combinations of food. Our only two restrictions were: nothing cooked, and nothing from animals. (Except honey. We used honey, because maple syrup is cooked for forty hours.)

When we were beginning our first "raw" week everyone in our family had a huge bowl of salad at each meal. I personally poured a half-cup of oil into mine. We were pleasantly surprised when our food consumption began to shrink during the second week, and went down to a quarter of the initial size by the end of the first month.

Now through the wisdom of our bodies we knew how much to eat and what to pick.

Valya: As soon as we returned from Michigan, we ordered a Vita-Mix blender, a dehydrator, and a Cuisinart processor. Our assortment of dishes increased a hundred times. We started to make seed cheese, pâté, nut milks, crackers. Sergei and I especially loved dessert. Our parents bought us some simple appliances at a garage sale. My brother and I burst into recipes!

We, as kids, were able to have fun creating our own dishes. Our friends loved to stay at our house. I was eight and Sergei was nine. Most kids at this age are not even allowed to use scissors. But we used knives, blenders and a dehydrator! Our friends enjoyed preparing food with us. I remember how they always asked, "Let's make something!"

One morning I was waiting for a school bus to come. Our neighbor Barbara saw me and started talking to me.

—Your mom looks really good. Is she on a new diet?
—Yes, we are all on a diet!
—What diet?
—It's a very good diet! We eat cookies, and cakes, and pies, and ice cream and candies.

In the evening Barbara was eating raw peach pie with us.

Running in
the Raw

Victoria: I read in a book *Reversing Diabetes* by
J. Whitaker that "exercise is a must for the
diabetic." I started to think about Sergei, that he
hardly exercised at all. Since we didn't put him on
insulin we had to make sure that we were doing
everything possible to heal his body. We understood
that exercising was fundamentally important for
Sergei. But how to make him do it?

Sergei: Mom told me that she and I would
start jogging every morning before school. She
knew that if she didn't start running with me I
wouldn't run. At the time we were both overweight,
and I was ashamed to run on the street; I thought
everybody would laugh at us. I had never run in
my life before. I imagined it would be super boring.

Very early in the morning when I was in the
most sound and sweet sleep Mom touched my arm.
To get out of my warm bed to go running seemed
unreal to me. It was still dark. But Mom was firm,
and I obeyed.

One minute after we started running we turned red as lobsters and were breathing as hard as water pumps. Two minutes later we couldn't run any more and needed to walk. Our poor fitness was frustrating, but it was going to change, because we enjoyed what we did. The morning air was fresh and clean. While walking back home we were watching the glorious sunrise. We felt happy. I decided to start running for myself, not for my diabetes.

Igor: I had been dreaming of running for years, but my poor body was chronically tired and it didn't have enough energy for running. After staying on raw food for several weeks I began to feel that my energy reserve was increasing.

Slowly but surely I started to run in the mornings. Our endurance was growing fast and soon we were participating in small races. We even won a few medals.

While running among other people, we noticed that they had to drink lots of electrolytes, or they would get dehydrated. They had many problems with blisters and foot and leg injuries. They had to load themselves with carbohydrates, or they wouldn't have enough energy and could lose too much weight. We had none of those problems. That must have been a result of a raw food diet.

Victoria: Once I called my doctor and told him that I was racing. He was horrified and told me that I had to stop running immediately, because I risked sudden death. His words scared me a lot and I decided not to call him anymore. I had a very strong feeling that I was now in charge of my life. Soon we cancelled our health insurance.

"Heavenly Enjoyment"

Victoria: After we had been on a raw food diet for six months, on my birthday I received a card from . . . myself. I looked at the invitation. It said: "Dear Victoria, happy birthday! You and your husband are cordially invited to come to our restaurant, you will be served clams, salmon, crab cakes"—everything I had picked. I had forgotten about this. The previous year in July I had decided to make a surprise for myself and prepaid for that birthday dinner at our favorite restaurant.

My brain began talking. "For six months we have been staying on 100 percent raw food like monks! We deserve a reward. This is my precious birthday! It's not a crime to eat cooked food once in six months! Come on! Everybody around us is eating mostly cooked food and nobody is dying!"

I asked Igor, "Can we just go and look? Or can we just bite it and spit it out?" Igor got excited. "Sure, let's go."

In the evening we tried to dress up; none of our old clothes fit us anymore.

We drove to the restaurant. It was so exciting to wait to be seated! We hadn't been in line in a restaurant for so long. Everything was so exciting, the

handsome waiter, the smell of the food, happy people
around us. Our waiter served us our food. It looked
delicious! It was going to be my best birthday!

After the first bite we thought we were in
Heaven! We felt high! We couldn't eat very much
now because our stomachs had shrunk from our
diet. Lots of food was left on the table. While leaving the restaurant both of us had a very bad after-
taste in our mouth. During the five-minute drive
home we began to feel sick. By the time we got
home we felt weak and nauseous and had to go to
bed. I knew it was from eating cooked food, but I
couldn't believe how severe it was.

Next morning I woke up with an already forgotten feeling of fatigue. When I saw myself in the
mirror I dropped the toothbrush. There were eye-
holes instead of eyes in my red, swollen face. I felt
dizzy. I wondered, "Where did my health achieve-
ments go?"

When I looked at my husband, I wanted to cry.
He showed me blood that was coming through the
skin under his knees. Igor's pulse was high, his
face was red, he felt shaky and miserable. He had
to cancel his work for the day. I said, "I am so
sorry, Igor, that I did this to you."

But the worst of all was the fact that we began
to crave cooked food so violently that our continuing to stay on a raw food diet was at great risk. It
took us many days to recover from our "heavenly
enjoyment" in the restaurant and go back to our
stable raw food living.

At first we didn't understand why other people could eat cooked food without any visible problem, and we, who actually were in great shape, got sick. Then we thought of healthy people who would get sick if they would smoke, or drink alcohol. Obviously, the human body builds up a protection against harmful substances. When human beings consume cooked food, their entire digestive tract is coated with a film of mucus. The more poisonous substances they consume, the thicker the mucous film becomes. The naturopaths call it "mucoid plaque." This is how the human body adjusts itself to the consumption of cooked foods.

This mucoid plaque protects our blood from absorbing dangerous substances. But at the same time mucoid plaque doesn't allow all the important nutrients to be utilized by the body. Hence people who eat mostly cooked food develop nutritional deficiencies.

In our case, Igor and I created a terrible shock for our bodies. We stayed for six months on a 100 percent raw vegan diet; our body trusted us and removed its mucous protection. And then we went "out" and consumed substances from which we were not protected anymore. As a result we got poisoned maybe 200 times more severely than anybody else at that restaurant. We've learned a very good lesson! Never ever will we do that again.

Many people, after staying on raw food for one or two months, get off it. I wish we all understood the importance of our behavior during this particular moment. Often we say: I became cold, I felt weak, I could not work, and so on. First of all, we don't have to explain anything to anybody. But if we want to share, we need to make sure we speak the truth. Then it makes sense. The most important is to keep the truth for our sake. Nothing is wrong with saying: It is hard, I could not make it; because then we have a chance to try again when we have better conditions. If we say raw food does not work, it doesn't fit me and so on, then we take the second chance away from ourselves. The fact that we breed fear and doubts about raw foods in other people does not hurt them as much as we hurt ourselves by closing the door to this most natural lifestyle.

Considering all this, I want to warn you. Don't become a raw fooder until you are absolutely ready for it. Maybe some of you are very excited and are ready to throw away pots and pans and to cover your stove with a huge cutting board. Sleep with this idea, get enough information. Be very careful. You are not just changing your wardrobe; you are changing your whole life.

I don't want you to do anything because I say so. If you want to change anything please change it because you feel it is right for you. Do you understand the difference?

Our Body Is Talking to Us

Victoria: There is nothing more important in the whole field of health, than to learn how to listen and understand our body. Our body is miraculously made. It can never make a mistake! It is always doing its best, trying to make us healthier! Sometimes we don't see it this way, because we don't understand our body's language.

When we are planning to travel to a foreign country we study the language of that country, so we don't get into trouble, or get lost. Similarly, if we don't understand the language of our own body, we can get in trouble. How can we learn our body's language?

When we started our raw food journey, I didn't know that every little feeling, every pain has an important message for us. I missed, or misinterpreted, most of those signs. I never let my body lead me. I used to think that my body is a dull matter.

I was very fat and very sick, and I didn't like my body. I thought that my body was very stupid

and it caused me only problems. My body gained
weight from whatever I ate, it craved bad things. It
created headaches, pains everywhere, and pimples
where I didn't want them to be. It couldn't run
without choking.

Now my body looks totally different, but it is
still the same body, it's me who changed. My body
always wanted to be healthier. It was me who was
ignorant and who always counteracted.

Now I am learning my body's language. The
more I learn, the more I discover how perfect my
body is.

For example, pain. I used to think that pain is
bad. It is like thinking that a fire alarm is bad. The
pain system in the human organism is a perfect
alarm system. Like the fire alarm demands that
we stop the smoke, the same way the pain in our
body is demanding to stop the wrongdoing. If we
have several pains, there are several wrongdoings.
As we don't destroy the alarm as it goes off, we
should not try to destroy the pain, but to fix the
cause.

Do you really think that your body creates the
pain to make you suffer?

Healthy people don't suffer from long-lasting
pains. When Sergei was snowboarding last winter he
broke his clavicle. The doctor in the emergency room
gave him a prescription for a pain killer. Sergei
refused to take it. The doctor told him that was very
silly, because everybody who breaks a clavicle goes
through unbearable pain during the first week.

Sergei brought pills home, but he never had to use them. As long as he stayed in a position that was best for the healing of a broken clavicle, it didn't hurt. But when he got tired of the same position and wanted to move, his body caused sharp pain, as if telling him, "Sorry, but you have to stay within these limits until I will repair your bone a little bit." His body was guarding him perfectly with a pain!

When we have a long-lasting pain, like toothache, or migraine, the most important message we should get from this pain is: "Stop eating!"

Perhaps you noticed that when you do have pain for several days, it usually hurts less in the morning, because you don't eat at night. In our family, whenever we had any pain we went on a water fast for just a couple of days, and it always worked!

If anybody in the world can heal our health problem, it's only our own body. All we need to do is to listen attentively to our organism so we can feel what kind of help our body wants from us. Maybe it wants us to fast on water, or to rest, or to eat certain fruit or to exercise.

Our body is constantly communicating with us by different sensations. Understanding the language of our own body is our best health insurance.

I used to think that the body was the lowest part of myself, and that the intellect has to control the body. Now I understand that it is just opposite. My intellect, (my image) is at the bottom and my

body is above. It is my bridge to the universe.
Through my body I am connected with God. My
body works according to universal laws. It is a part
of nature, and if I am in tune with my body, I can
know what is going on in the universe. My body
now helps me to understand everything. It's able to
get vibrations from other people and transmit them
to me and I sense them. Our body is a very miraculous thing.

When I began to observe my body very attentively I realized that every cell in my body knows
the future. My cells know what they will do tomorrow. They know what they will do in one year.
When I discussed this with Igor, my daughter
Valya was listening to us. Later I found a note on
the wall, that said: "How come every single cell is
so wise and all together it makes such an idiot?"

Economic Crisis

Victoria: While our family was experiencing positive changes on the plain of physical health, our financial side had a crack. Our local county found a zoning violation in our business operation, and after several hearings our business was shut down. We were quickly losing the ground under our feet. Our debts were growing. We were unable to sell our house due to zoning complications. Finally we were in foreclosure. We rented a storage unit and began to pack our books, kitchen appliances and other things.

Suddenly my brother called from Russia and told us that my mother was dying from cancer and she had maybe a couple of weeks left to live. I hadn't seen my mother for six years. I had to go, but I was afraid to travel to Russia alone. Igor and I flew to see my mother one last time, and our children stayed with our friends in the United States.

When we returned from Russia, we came just in time to watch the bulldozer smoothing out our oak furniture and other "treasures" in our former yard. While standing there and watching, I felt that my past life was also bulldozed over, pressed with all that wreck, and buried forever by the powerful machine.

We were homeless and unemployed now. That could be enough reason for someone to have a heart attack. But I was actually feeling relieved. Staying on raw food had transformed us. So we got our children and our dog into our Astrovan and hit the road. We did not have any other choice.

Living by Faith

Victoria: It seems that the universe is always providing us with a "no choice" situation whenever we need to go further, but are kind of stuck in a doorsill. I mean that we didn't want to go back and live like we used to live but we were afraid to make a real change, to start living by following our intuition, to live by faith. So we were pushed.

We had four hundred dollars in our pocket. Due to the type of visa that we had, we were not eligible to receive food stamps or other help from the American government.

We didn't know where we were going, for how long, what we were going to do, where we would end up, and we couldn't explain why we were going either. We surrendered.

For two and a half years we have been traveling around the United States. We put 200,000 miles on our van! Amazingly, our car never had any major problems during all this time. We went spontaneously from place to place. While preparing raw meals for one church we would get invited to do a presentation at a next-door senior center. At some places there were only five people, at others twenty. We collected only donations. Sometimes we made less money than we spent. Sometimes we got no money at all. Sometimes we earned good money. Once, a community in the Bahamas paid for our airplane tickets to the Bahamas, so we could teach them how to make tasty raw dishes. We learned that if we sincerely wanted to help, people gladly paid us.

When we did not have money we lived on sprouts and wild edibles. We always slept outside in free campgrounds, in different communities, or in our friends' backyards. We now had favorite places to stay in forty-nine states. We were sorry now that we had been "chained" to our house in Denver for so long. We had such a good life now! Every morning we ran, biked and swam. Then we spent time reading, writing letters, discussing our plans. After having a delicious lunch we worked for other people. Every night I read classical books aloud to my family. In the winter we moved towards Texas, Arizona, Florida. Once we spent a week on a deserted island in southern Florida.

In the summer we migrated towards spectacular Minnesota, Vermont, Maine. We lived like a royal family. We were relaxed and happy, no phone and TV, no appointments, deadlines or stress. We met many other people who lived this way. We had many opportunities to settle. We were offered good jobs at some health institutions. But we hadn't had enough of freedom yet.

Getting on the Path

Victoria: Once in the fall of 1997 we attended a gathering of long-distance hikers. They were sharing stories about their hikes and showing interesting slides. Then a sports nutritionist, whose specialty was long-distance hiking, advised hikers how to eat on the trail. His recommendations were alarming to us.

According to him, every hiker needs two pounds of M&Ms for every hundred miles, in order not to run out of energy halfway up the side of a mountain. Hikers need to snack every hour on an energy bar or candy in order "to head off those late-day energy crashes." He even suggested placing a chocolate bar under the pillow at night. Every time one awakens during the night one needs to take a bite. The average hiker loses 20 to 60 pounds of weight during a long-distance hike. It is a real problem and a reason for many hikers to drop off the trail prematurely. To avoid weight loss the doctor recommended to hikers that they "inhale a half-gallon of ice cream" every time they come into a new town.

We couldn't believe our ears! Instantly, we knew: this would be our next project. We had already been dreaming of crossing the country on foot for a while.

Now we had a mission too. We asked hikers how
much money they spent while hiking. The answer
was about $4,000 per person. They also told us it
usually takes about six months.

There are three major long-distance hiking
trails in the United States. We picked the Pacific
Crest Trail, 2,600 miles long. It starts on the
Mexican border, not far from San Diego. Then it
goes up north all the way to the Canadian border.

In December we headed across to San Diego.

The Raw Food Community of San Diego warmly
welcomed us. To raise money for our hike, they hired
us to prepare a raw dinner for over eighty members.
We got about $1,000. Some people traded backpacks
for Igor's massages. Jamie, from the Date People
Farm, supplied us with 4,500 medjool dates, five per
person per day for the entire hike. Our friend Wayne
Shelton volunteered to send us forty-two mail drops
along the trail. Local farmers provided us with dis-
counted nuts, seeds, figs and raisins. We bought ourselves Teva sandals; that was the only footwear we
had on the trail. We got detailed maps.

Everyday we practiced by hiking for two to four
hours in the mountains with pillows in our backpacks. We were getting ready to go.

Early in the morning on April 3, 1998, Wayne
took us to a trailhead. While the radio in the car
was promising a sunny weekend, it started to rain.
Wayne took our picture in front of the Mexican border monument, and we stepped into the rain.

Hiking without Cooking

From Valya's Diary:

*A*pr. 5. It seems that with every step I learn something new. Today we hiked thirteen miles, but my pack seems light. We're hiking well, and I'm warm. I hope that doesn't change!

Apr. 6. My ankle hurts and it's raining. Everything hurts! We just found out that our rainproof coats are not rainproof.

Apr. 7. We were hiking in the rain and got drenched. Our backpacks got waterlogged and very heavy. We knew that soon we would come to a big campground.

We are sitting on a big couch in the ranger's office, warming up by the fire. We hung our things to dry by the fireplace. There are bathrooms in this campground, hot showers and a roof. The mountains are beautiful here at Lake Marina. My mom and dad got four garbage bags from the rangers. It looks like these bags are going to be our rainproof coats from now on.

One of the hikers from a group we saw earlier is lost. There were three of them, and they lost the trail last night. Rangers found him after midnight. Andy had been alone in the forest for twenty eight hours, and he looked miserable! He was afraid he would starve to death. Andy says he will never hike again. Now he is waiting for his mom to pick him up. Meanwhile, the rangers are treating him with refried beans.

It's still raining and we are praying for it to stop.

Apr. 8. It was raining all night. I was hoping it would let up soon and it did! We continued our hike and picked miner's lettuce on the way. We had a wonderful dinner of miner's lettuce, one cucumber, half a carrot, oats and oil. We are really tired! It feels good to curl up in my warm dry sleeping bag.

Apr. 9. We woke up and it was so sunny that we put on shorts, short-sleeve T-shirts and went barefoot. Later we saw little chunks of snow on the ground. But the sun was so bright that we were sweating. Little by little, more and more snow appeared and soon there was snow everywhere. We surely would have lost the trail if someone hadn't left footprints in the snow. The snow was old and the little crystals were like glass cutting our feet.

We stopped to rest on a bare rock, and put on our sandals. We stepped in each other's footprints now because it was harder to make new ones. Every time I stepped I didn't know if I would sink deeper. My feet got colder with each step. The ice crystals stabbed my feet, and soon they felt like

solid rock. Finally my feet gave way, I mis-stepped
and fell in the snow. I burst into tears. I felt I
couldn't get up. Then my mother's arms pulled me
up. "We have to go," she said, and I went.

By now none of us could feel our toes. My dad
stopped and told us what to do. We stepped in the
nearby snowy stream. The water seemed warm to
our feet. We stayed in it until we began to feel
unbearable pain in our feet. Then we put on socks
and sandals, put out mats, and jogged in place.
Then we got out foot warmers and put black
garbage bags on our feet. Now our feet were warm.
We continued on. At dusk we crossed the road and
headed north.

We found a man and his family sledding. He said
we were going the wrong way! He kindly gave us a
ride to the post office, which was two miles away.

We found a store with apples, dried fruits, nuts
and oats. The lady who worked there gave us a
cabin, #12, with warm bath, a heater and beds.

When (my) dad took off his socks we looked at
his feet and froze. One foot was totally purple!
Mom suggested with a trembling voice, "Go wash it
first." When (my) dad came back, his foot was fine.
It turned out that the purple color came from the
plastic bag that he had had on his foot. Everybody
burst out laughing. We ate our food, which tasted
so good, and went to a warm, cozy bed. My dad
said we could have lost our toes.

Apr. 20. Today we are going through a desert.
It's so hot, the way I kept going was to imagine a

fresh, cold, juicy watermelon. My back is wet with sweat. It's like someone is testing me. Behind the road there is a creek and every time I step towards the road the road jumps away from me. It's like I'm walking on my nerves and my nerves are the trail.

Boy, if I thought I was hot before, I was wrong. Now I'm really hot! Then a miracle happened, we came upon a creek.

Apr. 21. Today we hiked through mountains, which had beautiful flowers. They're all so different, so colorful, so wonderful. I wish I had brought my pastels. The barrel cactuses were fat and thorny with a crown of yellow flowers on top. The thin cactuses have bright pink flowers and they taste better. The barrel cactuses taste like soft wood with lots of sour juice.

Apr. 22. We were hiking the big canyons in the San Felipe Mountains when it started raining. Once again, we were drenched and I got cold. But it was only my hands, so I stuck them in my short sleeves. We went around one mountain and came around to see yet another. I got so tired of constantly walking. I was soaked outside from rain and inside my "garby" (garbage bag) I was soaked from sweat. I felt that I could not take one more step and asked to stop and rest. But my father said that if we stop, we'll get hypothermia, and we could die. So, no matter how tired we are and no mater how far we have to go, we must keep moving.

And we kept hiking and the rain kept pouring.

My body finally went numb and I walked as if in a trance.

Suddenly we came to a fence and then the road. Finally, Warner Hot springs. We had hiked thirty-two miles that day, and a hundred feet to the hot swimming pool. When we got in that pool, we were the happiest people in the world that night.

Apr. 25. It feels good to have my pack on my back again.

We hiked all day to reach a campground. It was here that we met up with Gary, whom we had seen once before. He is hiking on crutches because he has diabetes. In his pack, he carries insulin for daily shots. And in the same pack he is carrying canned food, pots, pans and a small, but heavy stove.

Gary fell while crossing the last creek and severely twisted his knee. Since he was now abandoning the trail, he wanted us to take his food supplies. We thanked him, but didn't take any. Gary was sure that we were just shy. He brought us a box of expensive power bars, V-8 juice and chocolate bars. Mom just thanked him and took the box. We later gave it to a campground host.

In the morning we hiked two miles to a small town to buy some fruit at a local store.

When I look at food in the stores and see cakes and other cooked dishes, to me, they don't look like food, I don't relate them to things that I eat; they are just things that people look at. I know that it's food but I look at it as little toys that kids play with: the plastic pies and hamburgers, it looks like

that to me. When we go to stores, we go to the fruit
section and we go back out. As for the rest of the
store, we don't even know what it is filled with.
When I look at boxes of food, it looks like empty
cardboard boxes with different pictures.

Apr. 26. We hiked to a beautiful wild hot
springs; I swam the whole day! The next day I
woke up and went swimming again. I didn't even
eat breakfast, so my mom brought Sergei and me
some tea and dates. Our plates whirled round in
the pool. Swim, swim, take a sip. Swim, swim, eat
a date. It felt good. It was our last day and I did
not want to leave and possibly never return. But it
would be fun to start hiking again.

Apr. 30. Our 13-year-old friend Naomi joined us
for three days. We took it easy and hiked only six
miles in deference to Naomi. Dad still had bound-
less energy; he jogged all the way to where we
started that day and back. Naomi didn't eat our
wild salad, but she ate all of the food that she had:
salted peanuts, three power bars and candy.

May 1. We each had three medjool dates and
water for breakfast. We don't usually eat until 3
p.m., because after lunch it's much harder to hike.
When Naomi tried our lunch (wild onion, miner's
lettuce, oats and oil) she said, "I am sick of your
food, I hate it, I'm tired of oats." My mom asked
her what would she eat. Naomi closed her eyes and
said, "Maybe an apple, or banana."

Later we were hiking through a small campground when we saw a group of people having a

picnic. They had two green apples and two bananas on the table. My parents asked them if they would trade fruit for a Russian Deep Tissue Massage. One man agreed and Naomi got her wish.

Tomorrow is Naomi's last day with us. We have eight miles before we meet her parents at the road.

May 2. Soon after we set out, the temperature rose quickly. It seemed it would never end. Naomi was hungry and dragging. I found a horseradish leaf and gave it to her. Soon she asked for more. She said she would eat anything, perhaps even garbanzo beans.

For dinner we had a beautiful salad made with wild celery, wild turnip leaves, wild onions, and yellow mustard flowers. We used a pinch of raw rolled oats with water and kelp for dressing (Dad had used the oil for the massage). It was delicious. Naomi said she never tasted better food in her life and had two plates!

We finally made it to the road and who was there but her parents with a basket of sweet organic strawberries waiting for us. Naomi was tired and hurting, but smiling.

She kept singing:
"Miner's lettuce is so yummy,
I just want it in my tummy."

That evening, we sat around the fire and chewed dates. Sergi got bitten by twenty ants and had to soak his feet in the stream. We sat around the fire and laughed at my dad's poem about a forest tick that he made up in Russian.

May 6. It was a steep climb all day. We logged eighteen miles and we went through endless fields of flowers. Orange poppies, bright pink, yellow, white, red and purple flowers, all sizes, and everywhere!

We passed right to the desert, but it was surprisingly cold.

As time passed it got warmer and then hotter. We took breaks under the Joshua trees.

We tried a shortcut but got lost. We had to hike back more than seven miles. We worried that we would not reach the post office before it closed for a three-day weekend.

To my surprise, the cities are so boring. No matter what I do, it does not feel right. I even went to the park and swung on the swings, which is my favorite thing to do, and that didn't help. I cannot wait to start hiking again.

May 10. It is a very, very windy day. We hiked a white mountain made of chalk. I even drew with it. The next mountain was made up of all different kinds of rock in one. It was a beautiful day.

May 19. It is raining in the mountains. We are stuck at the same campsite for the third day already. Usually when it rained we would hike all the way to civilization without a single break. But this is different because we are forty miles away from anything.

May 20. In the morning I got out of my warm, soft, cozy sleeping bag into the cold fog. Everyone was hurrying and stuffing everything into their packs. After the short pleasure of breakfast we were off. We have been in every weather but fog and now we were in that, too!

We hiked through the tall wet grass with our shorts so we don't get our pants wet. I like the fog. There is something mystical in it.

It took us all day to reach Sierra City where we found a beautiful campground. Mom and dad went to the post office while we kids stayed in the woods. I sat on a flat rock that was a perfect seat. I was a little scared because what if I saw a bear? But I calmed myself. Black bears don't eat people; they just want hiker's food. But I have honey in my stomach. What if they can smell me? But we haven't seen any yet, so we probably won't see any.

I was writing letters to my pen pals when I heard a sound like rocks falling. I turned around and there he was: big wet black bear. He was beautiful. So swift but yet so clumsy. His fur was wet so I knew that he had just swum the river. He passed within twenty feet without even looking at me. Only after he passed I understood: I saw a bear.

The sun is warming the earth, the sky has not a single cloud and the birds are singing everywhere. In front of me is an ocean of mountains to climb. When I climb a mountain I never know what is on the other side, a jeep road, a city or just another mountain to climb. Just like in real life.

Ashland

Victoria: When we reached Ashland, there was forty feet of snow on the trail and we could not continue. Forty feet of snow was just too much! We could not see the trail, and we had already been lost several times. The rangers told us that they didn't want to look for us in helicopters, so we had to wait in Ashland for at least six weeks before the snow would melt and it would be safe to return to the trail. It was a tough situation. We had only five dollars. Our next mail drop was waiting for us sixty miles ahead at Crater Lake Post Office. We couldn't live in town for six weeks without money.

While hiking through Ashland we came across beautiful Lithia Park. We swam in the river, had salad with wild greens and camped overnight in the nearby forest.

In the morning we began talking to people that we met in the park and getting information about possible trades. We were offering garden work in exchange for a place to camp. Several people mentioned WellSprings: "They have recently had a bad flood and there is a lot of cleaning to be done."

A couple of hours later we were entering WellSprings.

The very first man that we met appeared to be the owner of the WellSprings, Gerry. We had an amazing conversation:

—Would you like some help in exchange for free camping?
—The only help we need is in the kitchen.
—We cannot work in the kitchen.
—Why?
—We are on a special diet.
—What diet?
—Raw food.
—I cannot believe it! We have organized an education kitchen and have been looking for a chef through the entire spring. We couldn't find anybody except tofu-dog chef and finally, yesterday, we were standing in a circle and praying to God to send a raw food chef our way. And here you are! I cannot wait to try some of your food!

We went to the local health store and Gerry bought everything that we told him to buy. Then Gerry took us to the beautiful kitchen with its Vita-Mix blender, Champion juicer, processor, trays for growing sprouts and very sharp knives.

We made borscht, nutmeat cutlets, hummus and cake. Gerry and his friends loved everything. He handed us a key and a checkbook and said, "Do whatever you want here, I'm sure it will work well."

We had a wonderful time working at Springs

*Garden Café! Every morning we picked fresh greens
and fresh vegetables from the organic garden in the
back of the WellSprings. We prepared beautiful live
food. We swam in the healing mineral waters. We
were surrounded by many like-minded people. We
met many new friends.*

Meanwhile the snow on the trail had melted
and we were committed to finish our hike. So we
packed and left to continue our journey on the
Pacific Crest Trail.

As soon as we left something happened that
had never happened to us before. Our hearts were
telling us, "You have just left your home! You need
to be back!"

The Happy End or the Happy Beginning?

Victoria: We reached the Canadian border on September 16, 1998, on a stormy day. We had to run the last ten miles in the darkness in order to reach the shelter in the Canadian state park.

There's really no way to describe a thru-hike to others. What to tell? That Sergei had 174 ticks? None of which bit him! Or that Valya met a bear one-on-one in the Sierras? That I crawled on my knees four miles on a fragile crust of mushy snow? But we mention those things just for the effect, they are not important. The real treasures are hard to explain. The greatest thing we understood on the trail was that we don't need a lot to be happy.

Our craving for traveling was over. We clearly wanted to return to Ashland and to start living there.

And so we did. Gerry helped us to buy a trailer right at our favorite WellSprings. Everything fell into place. We live now in the town of our dreams. In order to find it we had to search in every corner of the United States for almost three years and to cross the country on foot. Sometimes we wonder, "What if we had never hiked the Pacific Crest Trail? What if we never left Denver? What if we never went on raw food?"

Sergei's Teen Message

I am so lucky that I am a raw fooder, because I am cured of my diabetes. I will never ever have to worry about getting sick with any life-threatening illness, no matter how serious it may be. I will never ever have to worry about any kind of Y2K problems in the future, for I know how to survive in the woods without any food for long periods of time.

I used to be deadly afraid of spiders and of death but I no longer have to worry about either. Raw food helped me to get rid of all fears.

Several years ago I used to be so petrified of death. I wouldn't be able to go to sleep some nights because I would be thinking: we sure live for a long time, but it's not even a second as long as we are going to be dead. It's like we are going to be dead forever and we live for only a half a second. This would scare me so much because I was attached to my body and to material things. It was incredibly scary to think of things like that.

In time I realized I shouldn't be scared anymore because just like birth is wonderful, death is wonderful too. I don't really truly believe anymore that we die because, one time at the Creative Health

Institute in Michigan, there was a guy named
Mike. He was carried in by four big men. The doctors told him that he had two days to live. He
couldn't walk or do anything. So he was put onto
the bed. We started giving him wheat grass and he
started fasting. The miracle happened! Mike started walking within a month. He started working,
helping to mow the lawn on the tractor. In three
months he was running in the mornings, he was
going down the river with me in a river raft. He
was really active and really happy. For the first
time in his life he said he was really happy.

Mike used to drink a lot, so only one percent of
his liver was working. After three months Mike felt
so excellent, that he decided that he was cured,
and he went out and had a prime rib dinner with a
girlfriend. That night he died.

When my parents went to the hospital that
night they took me with them "to say goodbye to
Mike." And I looked at his body and I touched his
body. It was like a piece of skin. There was no soul
in it. It was just like a doll, it wasn't even human.

Since then I know that we don't really die, we
go somewhere else but we don't really die. Maybe
that was the last step I had to take to realize that
we shouldn't be scared of death.

I no longer have to worry about fitting into any
kind of group or culture because when I became a
raw fooder I stopped caring what others think about
me. I am not afraid of poverty anymore nor am I
afraid of starving to death because I know that it's

not possible. Now I am no longer scared to live.

I started liking to work when I became a raw fooder. Before when my mom asked me to do something, I'd always do it the easiest way and as fast as I could. If she asked me to sweep the floor, I would sweep the dirt under the rug. If she asked me to wash the dishes, I would just rinse them, like put them under the water. I hated work. In the summer I used to sit all the time on our couch, and not do anything. My friends and I would be bored for three months and we couldn't think of anything to do.

After about a year into raw food, I wouldn't be able to enjoy a TV show knowing there was a big pile of dishes to be washed. I started to like working and realized that without work, life is boring.

Before I went on raw food I was below average in school. I was a class clown and I never did my homework. I was always hyperactive and I couldn't sit still. The teachers were thinking of holding me back because I wasn't reading well enough.

When I started eating raw food in the middle of fourth grade, I turned into one of the top ten kids in the class. It was interesting because in the first half of the year I was the worst student and in the last half I was one of the best students. The principal himself gave me an award and said he had never seen this happen before. My grades went up. There was a startling difference. I was no longer a 'D' student, I was an 'A' or 'B' student. I was able to listen to the teacher and enjoy what he was saying, and enjoy the process.

School became so simple that I dropped out and home-schooled, doing two grades in one year. That became easy and I decided to skip high school. I took the placement test at the college and scored well. Now I am going to a community college in Medford. I am 15 years old. I have a 'B' average in college. I am pretty happy about that.

My relationships with other people changed. Now I attract different kinds of people, those who share my beliefs. But the friends that I had before, the true friends, they stuck with me.

When I watch my friends having to wear glasses and braces and getting sick often, having mood swings, I feel very sorry for them. I wish I could tell them all that they don't need to suffer. But I know that most of them wouldn't listen to a word I say. I know that the only thing I can do is be a good example. They might never figure out that there are other ways of dealing with their problems. They might never figure this out because wherever they are they receive false information. In school, they always hear that if you are sick, take a pill. They hear it on TV, from parents, and from friends. That's why some friends might be skeptical when I tell them that if you're raw you have nothing to fear. You will never get sick and if you do, raw food will cure you.

I wish I could tell my friends' parents that it's very important that they become at least somewhat raw. Their children are counting on them.

Maybe the parents aren't sick but if the kids are, then there is no better reason to become a raw fooder. Such a child will have a happy, fruitful life. He/she will never want to try drugs; any drug will seem very dumb and unnecessary because a raw fooder's life is already filled with events and feelings that create a sort of "natural high."

If many more children go on a raw food diet the world will become a better, cleaner, healthier place to live.

Even if people just stop eating meat, there will be a great deal more trees. More trees means cleaner air. Cleaner air means healthier people.

My parents made it easier for me and my sister to stay on raw food by getting us our own appliances: blender, food processor, knives and so on. That made it easier because we, as kids, were able to have fun creating our own dishes. But even more importantly they made it easier for me because they themselves were a good example. They never cheated no matter how hard it became. This showed me in a sense how much raw food meant to them. Since we are a family, I too started helping my parents by being a good example and never cheating. In no time we had a sort of cycle going; when one of us was having a hard time the others would do the best they could to help. It's easier to be successful when you have support.

My parents changed a lot from this diet. First they stopped fighting in general. Then they became a great deal nicer, more open. It is easier to talk to

my parents now, knowing that they only want to
help me with my problems, not judge me. My parents now give me a lot of freedom, they never
ground me, or suppress me. They believe that they
don't own me, that I own myself. Therefore they
never force me to do something I don't want to do.
Even when I'm doing something they don't approve
of, they never stop me from learning a lesson on
my own.

I feel that eating raw food is the right thing to
do and that is why I do it, not because my parents
tell me to do it. My parents are really open. They
don't say, "No, you can't eat cooked food." If I wanted to eat cooked food I would eat it. But I realize
on my own that I don't really want to eat it. I am
really happy that they introduced me to raw food.
I hope that anyone who has kids can talk to them
about it or just be a good example. Being an example is the number one way of teaching people.

My sister, mom, dad and I all sleep outside. We
have a house but only our dog sleeps there. We
built ourselves a little enclosed area outside so we
could sleep and breathe fresh air. I know that
breathing fresh air brings me great health. I
noticed that when I sleep outside I always have a
deep peaceful sleep like a baby, I need less sleep,
and I recover better from a hard day's work.

One winter we lived in a small cabin for a little
while. The first thing I had to do in the morning
was to build a fire because it was incredibly cold.
Chopping wood at dawn woke me up.

Two or three times when we traveled we had to
sleep in a motel because of the weather. In the
morning I always felt so heavy, as if I had eaten
some cooked food. My mom always has a headache
when she sleeps indoors. We try to sleep outside
now even when the weather is really bad. For
example, in the rain we cover ourselves with a
tarp. I like what Peace Pilgrim said about it: "We
are not made out of sugar, therefore we cannot
melt."

Also we don't have beds, instead we sleep on
hard wood floors because we feel it's right.

When we lived in Denver my friends would
come over to my house a lot and jump on my soft
bouncy bed. As time went on, our thinking started
to change and we came around to sleeping on hard
surfaces. My dad cut hard oak boards and placed
them over each one of our beds. When my friend
Stephen came over the next day, he tried a face
plant on my no longer soft bed and almost broke
his nose.

Often people ask me if I crave pizza, chips or
any other popular "teen food." I don't remember
eating cooked food at all; it has been a while since I
ate cooked foods and even the concept of warm food
seems weird to me. Why would I want to heat
something and stick it into my mouth?

Some people share their concern that we can't
be social on raw food. I think that that's a false
theory. Every restaurant would serve you a salad.
If they don't have a salad, ask them to bring you

sliced zucchini, or tomato, or carrot, or onion, or
any vegetable that they have, without any dressing
on it. Ask them if they have olive oil. Always have
a little shaker of Mrs. Dash, or kelp, or Spike, or
other seasoning in your car for such occasions.

When we have an appointment at a restaurant
we bring a big watermelon with us, give it to the
chef and ask him cut it up for us nicely. When the
waiter brings cut watermelon on a beautiful tray,
our friends forget completely about what they
ordered, because fresh watermelon looks so much
better then the picture of the hamburger. The
watermelon always seems to go first. Then we give
both the chef and waiter a $5 tip.

I began to eat way less on raw foods.
Sometimes when I go out to a restaurant with my
friends I just get some tea or not even that.
Sometimes I am not hungry. I just sit and talk to
my friends as they are eating their food. Though I
don't think they understand.

I noticed that after about two years of being
100 percent raw I started eating really simply. I no
longer wanted any gourmet food; a simple salad
started to seem one hundred times better. I seem to
have come closer to nature. Now I enjoy eating
whole foods like a carrot or an apple, more then I
enjoy eating a fancy cake. I am not saying you
should stop eating beautiful gourmet raw food,
instead what I am saying is listen to your body and
eventually you might come to eat simpler.

I don't get sick anymore but once in a while I

get something called a healing crisis because it
takes seven years to fully cleanse the body.
Medicine takes the longest to get out of the body.
Every once in a while I get a healing crisis. It is a
type of cleansing that comes suddenly and goes
suddenly. You never know when to expect a healing
crisis.

Not to scare the reader, healing events are
actually a wonderful thing. In fact you should be
worried if you don't get them because that means
you might have a serious health problem.

When someone stays on a raw food diet for even
a short period of time their awareness increases. A
well-aware person would never ever hurt anyone or
anything. One will instead concentrate on improv-
ing one's own self, and by so doing that person
inspires other people to change the way they live.
Can you imagine how much a group of twenty
inspired people could do?

Raw food is not the most important thing in
life. In my opinion the most important thing in life
is to be free. Being free means being happy. When
you're happy you're not attached to anything or
anybody. You can be happy on top of a mountain
by yourself or you can be happy in a traffic jam.
Though raw food is not the most important thing
in life, I still see it as very important, because raw
food gives people the energy they need to achieve
true freedom.

Science or Intuition?

Victoria: There is no knowledge more important than the knowledge of listening to our body for the sake of our own health. We have an illusion that somebody from the outside can heal us. If anybody in the world can heal us, it is only ourselves. It will take centuries for science to learn the hopelessness of the attempt to push the everchanging human body into frames of scientific theories. But it is possible to know what we need to do here and now for our health. It is possible to learn how to hear our body's voice.

When I started to use my intuition, I knew that I always have had it and I know that everybody else has it. Everybody is born with intuition. It is our human nature to have intuition.

Instead of making an effort to memorize the information, we should try better to hear the message from our own body.

Sometimes the cooked foods advocates blame raw fooders with lacking a scientific foundation. The most paradoxical is the fact that raw foodism does not need scientific explanation, because it just works.

Staying on raw food successfully does not depend

on the amount of our knowledge but from the faith in nature and our organism.

Scientifica sounding theories create fear in us that we cannot be raw fooders successfully. We can get disappointed and step back. Like I did for many years.

I was conditioned to such a point that, until six years ago, I was not able to say anything for my own self. I was always looking for solutions in a book. Whatever I said was what I read somewhere else or heard from somebody who "knows better" than I do. I was thinking that whatever I say from myself doesn't have any value. I hope you understand that because many people have gone through the same stages in their lives.

I thought I could never say anything that has never been said before. I was sure that everything I knew came to me from other books and from other people.

Then I discovered that I do know things I never heard and I do have freedom to see and decide for myself.

Valya's Dreams

Imagine a world full of raw fooders. Wouldn't it be wonderful to be around such healthy people? Because when people are healthier, they tend to be much happier.

I went on raw food to be healthier but now I do it to be happier. When I eat raw food I feel free, and thus happier. I love feeling happy. Don't you? I think that happiness is the most important thing in life. Have you noticed that when you are happy it makes everything seem wonderful? As wonderful as the stars in the sky.

Often we think, let the world become raw first and then I will. It would be so much easier then. It would. That's why by being a raw fooder you help the rest of the world to do it.

Wouldn't it be great if instead of ice cream trucks there would be frozen wheat grass Popsicle trucks. Billboards, instead of promoting hamburgers, would show fresh organic durians. Or maybe there would not be any billboards. Maybe raw food would help clear our minds and make us more conscious. Then maybe there would be less pollution. Then the planet would be happy too!

Recipes

Thai Salad

4 cucumbers
Juice of 1 lemon
1 bunch dill
1 bunch cilantro
1 medium onion diced
2 teaspoons hot curry powder
2 teaspoons turmeric powder
1 teaspoon salt (or to taste)
3 Tablespoons honey
1/3 cup olive oil
The meat of one young coconut diced
1 cup sunflower seeds (soaked for 2 hours)

Peel and slice the cucumbers into thin circles and transfer to a bowl. Thinly dice meat of coconut. Finely chop the cilantro and dill and mix with the cucumbers. Add the onion, lemon juice, and olive oil. Finish by adding the rest of the ingredients and mixing well.

Serves 5-8

I Can't Believe It's Just Cabbage Salad

1 head white cabbage
5 Tablespoons olive oil
5 Tablespoons lemon juice
1 teaspoon salt (optional)
1 Tablespoon nutritional yeast

Mix all ingredients in a bowl and decorate with your favorite herb.

Serves 3-5

Kale Salad

2 bunches curly kale, chopped
1 bunch radishes, thinly sliced
1/2 head cauliflower, diced
1/2 head white cabbage, sliced
1/4 cup olive oil
6 Tablespoons apple cider vinegar
1 teaspoon salt (optional)
2 Tablespoons honey or anything else that's
    sweet: apple juice, date paste, etc.

Mix all the vegetables in a bowl. Add in the remaining ingredients and mix well.

Serves 7-9

Generic Recipe for Dressing

Blend the following in a blender until smooth:

Oil (any good oil such as sesame, olive, flax).
  Use enough to cover the blades of the
  blender.

1 teaspoon honey (or any other natural sweet-
  ener, like raisins or bananas)

5 Tablespoons fresh lemon juice (or lime juice or
  apple cider vinegar)

1/3 cup water

1 cup chopped fresh herbs (celery, parsley,
  cilantro, basil, etc.)

Spice to taste (garlic, mustard, ginger, jalapeno,
  etc.)

1/3 cup seeds or nuts (the most common are
  sunflower seeds and tahini; also: walnuts,
  pumpkin seeds, almonds, etc.)

1/2 teaspoon salt (optional)

Don't be afraid to improvise. You may sometimes
add more liquid, or skip one ingredient completely.
If it tastes good, put it in. Good luck!

Serves 7-10

Pesto Dressing

1/4 cup olive oil
5 cloves garlic
1/2 cup pine nuts
1 bunch fresh basil
1/4 cup lemon juice
1 teaspoon salt (optional)

Blend in a blender thoroughly.   *Serves 4-5*

Cream of Celery Soup

1 large bunch celery
4 cups water
1/4 cup olive oil
1/4 cup lemon juice
2 teaspoons honey or raisins
Spicy pepper to taste
1-2 teaspoons sea salt

Blend all ingredients in a blender until fine.

Add:
1 chopped avocado
1 small sweet red pepper, chopped
1/2 bunch parsley chopped
2 carrots or parsnips grated

Serves 6

Borscht

Blend these ingredients well in a blender or Vitamix:
    2 cups water
    3 beets
    1 small root ginger (sliced)
    3-4 large cloves garlic
    6-7 bay leaves

Pour the mixture into a big bowl. Blend the following ingredients for a short time (about 30 seconds):
    2 cups water
    2 carrots
    2 stalks celery
    2 Tablespoons apple cider vinegar
    3-4 oranges, peeled with the seeds out (seeds
        will make a very bitter taste)
    2 Tablespoons honey
    1/4 cup olive oil
    Sea salt to taste (optional)

Add 1/2 cup walnuts and blend on low speed very quickly so that they break into small pieces but are not blended. Pour in the same bowl and stir.

Dice or grate:
    1/4 head cabbage
    1-2 carrots
    1 bunch parsley

Add grated ingredients to the blended mixture. Stir and serve.   *Serves 7-10*

Generic Recipe for Chowder

Blend 1 cup of any nuts (soaked overnight) with 2 cups of water to a creamy consistency. Add the rest of the following and blend well:

    1 cup water
    1/2 cup extra virgin olive oil
    1 teaspoons honey
    1 cup chopped celery
    Hot peppers to taste
    2-5 cloves garlic
    1 teaspoon salt (optional)

Now you have plain chowder. You pick the flavor:

    For clam-chowder taste add: dulse flakes
    For broccoli: chopped broccoli
    For mushroom: your favorite mushrooms, dry
       or fresh
    For tomato: chopped tomato
    For carrot: grated carrots
    For corn: cut corn off the cob
    For pea: fresh peas
    Your own creation . . .

Sprinkle with dry parsley flakes before serving. Note: this soup will become warm because of much blending. It's still raw. (Just don't let it become hot!) Warm soups are comforting in the cold wintertime.

Serves 5

Gazpacho

Blend the following ingredients in a blender until smooth:

　　1/2 cup water
　　1/4 cup extra virgin olive oil
　　5 large ripe tomatoes
　　2 cloves garlic or spicy pepper to taste
　　1 Tablespoon raw honey (dates or raisins work
　　　　just as well)
　　6 Tablespoons lemon juice
　　1 teaspoon sea salt (optional)
　　1 bunch of fresh basil

Now that you have the gazpacho liquid, cut the following vegetables into 1/2 inch cubes:

　　1 large avocado
　　1 medium bell pepper
　　5 sticks celery
　　1 small white onion

Mix all ingredients in a bowl and sprinkle with chopped parsley.　　　　　　　*Serves 4*

Live Garden Burger

Grind 1 pound of your favorite nuts in a food
processor. Combine the following ingredients and
grind in a food processor or put through a
Champion Juicer with the blank plate:

    1 pound carrots
    1 medium onion
    2 Tablespoons sweetener (honey, very
        ripe banana, raisins)
    3 Tablespoons oil
    1-2 Tablespoons poultry seasoning (or other
        seasoning)
    1/2 Sea salt (optional)

*If the mixture is not firm enough, add one or more
of the following thickeners: dried dill weed, dried
garlic powder, dried onion powder, dried parsley
flakes, nutritional yeast, psyllium husk powder, or
ground flaxseeds. With garden burger you can make
nori rolls, cabbage wraps, spread it on crackers,
stuff mushrooms, peppers, tomatoes, onions, cucumbers, and more.*

Serves 10

Nori Rolls

Paté mixture:
  1/2 cup walnuts
  2 cups sunflower seeds, soaked overnight
  3 garlic cloves
  1 cup chopped celery
  1 teaspoon salt (optional)
  1/3 cup olive oil
  1/4 cup lemon juice
  1 teaspoon curry powder (or your favorite
    seasoning)

Additional ingredients: Slice into long, thin strips
the following:
  1/2 avocado
  1/2 large bell pepper
  2 green onions

Blend all the paté ingredients in a food processor
until creamy. Spread the paté onto a sheet of nori.
Place the thinly sliced vegetables on the pate. Roll
up tightly in nori sheet. Note: to make the nori
sheets stick better you can moisten them a little
with water, lemon, tomato, or orange juice. Let the
nori rolls sit for 10 minutes and then begin slicing
them into 2-inch slices.

Makes 10-15 nori rolls

Worthy Guacamole

Blend the following ingredients in a food processor:
- 3 large RIPE avocados
- 1 teaspoon sea salt
- 4 Tablespoons lemon juice
- 4-8 cloves garlic (depending on how much you like garlic)

Chop the following ingredients:
- 1 medium tomato
- 1/4 medium onion
- 1/2 bunch cilantro

Mix all ingredients in a bowl and sprinkle with chili pepper if desired. Eat on top of crackers, or wrap into cabbage or nori. Fill lettuce or simply eat with a spoon.

Serves 4-6

Valya's Spicy Almond Cheese

Mix the following ingredients in a bowl:
 2 cups pulp from almond milk (pulp should not
   be sweet)
 1/4 cup olive oil
 1/4 cup lemon juice
 1/2 teaspoon salt (optional)
 1/2 bunch fresh or dried dill weed
 1/2 cup diced onions
 1/2 cup diced red bell pepper

Decorate with cherry tomatoes.   *Serves 4*

Sergei's Hummus

Blend the following ingredients in a food processor:
  2 cups garbanzo beans, sprouted for 1 day
  1/4 cup extra virgin olive oil
  2 chopped carrots
  1 cup tomatoes, chopped
  1 cup celery, chopped
  1/2 teaspoon salt (optional)
  1/4 cup fresh dill or basil
  4 Tablespoons lime or lemon juice
  Hot peppers to taste
  2-5 cloves garlic

Sprinkle with dry parsley flakes before serving.

Serves 5-7

Crunch Fries with Ketchup

Crunch Fries:
Slice 1 pound of jicama so it looks like French fries.
Combine in a bowl with:
> 2 Tablespoons onion powder
> 2 Tablespoons extra virgin olive oil
> Sea salt to taste (optional)
> 1 Tablespoon paprika

Ketchup:
Blend the following ingredients in a blender until smooth:
> 1/2 cup dried tomatoes, soaked for 2 hours
> 4 Tablespoons apple cider vinegar
> 1/4 cup raisins
> 1/4 cup onion powder
> 1/2 teaspoon salt (optional)
> 1/2 cup water

Serves 5

Pickles

Ingredients:

    3 lbs pickling cucumbers
    1/2 big bunch of Pickling dill (with seeds)
    4 horseradish leaves (for crunchiness)
    1 medium head garlic
    6 cups of water
    9 Tablespoons of sea salt

Cut one quarter of an inch off both ends of pickling cucumbers. Stuff the cucumbers into a glass gallon jar with garlic, dill (with seeds), and fresh horseradish leaves. If you have hard time finding horseradish leaves, you may use grape, currant or cherry leaves instead.

Mix the water and salt in a blender:

Pour the salt-water into the gallon jar so that the pickles are covered. If needed, add plain water to completely submerge the pickles. Let this jar sit on the counter covered with a cloth for two days. On the third day the pickles will be pickled enough to eat. If you will decide after four or five days that you want them to stop pickling, drain the water, cover the jar with lid and place them in the refrigerator.

Raw Family's Green Juice

Blend these ingredients well in a blender:
    1 large bunch kale, chopped
    2 medium apples, chopped
    1/2 lemon with peel, chopped
    1 cup water

Strain the liquid through a nut-milk bag or sprouting bag.

Serves 3-4

Nut or Seed Milk

    1 cup any nuts or seeds, soaked overnight
    3 cups water
    1 Tablespoon honey or 2-3 dates
    1 teaspoon Celtic salt (optional)

Thoroughly blend all ingredients in a blender until smooth. Strain mixture through a sprout bag, and then drink.

Serves 4

Simple Crackers

　　2 cups whole flax seed
　　1 cup water
　　1/2 teaspoon salt (optional)

If you want to enhance the flavor, blend in a bunch
of your favorite herbs and/or a tomato.

　　Mix and spread one-inch thick with a spatula
on dehydrator sheets. Dehydrate for about 12 hours
or until crisp.

Yields 16 crackers

Igor's Crackers

Grind 2 cups of flaxseed in a dry Vitamix container.
Blend together:

    1 cup water
    1 large onion, grated
    3 stalks celery, grated
    4 cloves garlic, medium
    2 tomatoes (optional)
    1 teaspoon caraway seed
    1 teaspoon coriander seed
    1 teaspoon Celtic salt (optional)

Mix ground flaxseed into blended mix by hand.
Dough should be slimy not dry. Cover the dough
with cheesecloth or a towel and let sit in a bowl at
a warm room temperature overnight to ferment
slightly. If more sour taste is desired, ferment 2-3
days. Using a spatula spread on non-stick dehy-
drating sheets. Divide into squares of desired size.
For softer bread, dehydrate 16 hours on one side, 4
hours on the other. For crispy crackers, dry well.
Keep crackers refrigerated.

Yields 16 crackers

Dried Veggie-Burgers

Grind 1 pound of flaxseed in a Vita-Mix without adding water. Grind 1 pound of your favorite nuts in a food processor.

Combine the following ingredients in the bowl and mix with your hands well.

> 1 pound carrot pulp (from juice)
> 1 medium onion, grated
> 2 Tablespoons sweetener (honey, very ripe
>   banana or raisins, blended with a little
>   water to the consistency of honey)
> 3 Tablespoons oil
> 1-2 jalapenos or other spice to taste
> 1/2 Sea salt (optional)

Mix well. You have to experiment to get the desired consistency. Shape into burgers using ice-scream scoop and put on dehydrator sheets. Dehydrate at 105-115 degrees for several hours; approximately 10 hours on one side, and then flip for 3 hours on opposite side.

Serves 10

Banango Smoothie

Blend the following ingredients in a blender until smooth:
    2 frozen bananas
    1 1/2 cups frozen mango chunks (add more if
        desired)
    1 cup orange juice

Cut up one fresh ripe mango into small cubes and mix into each cup for texture.

Serves 2-3

Green Smoothie

Blend the following ingredients in a blender until smooth:
    4 pears or peaches or nectarines
    1 banana
    1 peeled orange
    1 handful of greens (parsley, romaine, etc.)
    1 cup water

Blend the following ingredients in a blender until smooth.

Serves 2-3

Generic Cake Recipe

Crust
Grind the following ingredients in a food processor, and mix well:

    1 cup nuts, or seeds
    1/2 cup dried fruit such as: raisins, dates, figs,
        prunes, bananas, dried apricots, etc.
    1/4 salt (optional)
    1 teaspoon vanilla

If mixture is not firm enough, add psyllium husk, or shredded coconut. Form into crust on a flat plate.

Topping
Blend the following ingredients well, and add water if needed:

    1/2 cup nuts (white nuts such as macadamia
        nuts, cashews, and pine nuts, make a white
        toping)
    2-3 Tablespoons honey (or sweet dried fruit)
    2 Tablespoons lemon Juice
    1 teaspoon vanilla

Spread topping evenly over the crust. Decorate with fruits, berries, and nuts. Give your cake a name. Chill.

Serves 8

Walnut Cream Cake

Crust

Grind the following ingredients in a food possessor, and mix well:

    1 cup walnuts
    1 cup raisins
    1 teaspoon vanilla
    1/2 teaspoon salt (optional)
    1 Tablespoon ground lemon zest.

Form into crust on a flat plate. Make a layer of fresh sliced fruit such as bananas pears, or peaches. Form another layer of crust over this.

Topping

Blend the following ingredients well; add water if needed:

    1/2 cup walnuts
    1/4 cup water
    2-3 Tablespoons raw honey
    2 tablespoons lemon Juice
    1/4 teaspoon salt (optional)
    1/3 teaspoon nutmeg (optional)

Spread evenly over the crust. Decorate with fruits, berries, and nuts. Chill.

Serves 12

Un–Chocolate Cake

Crust
Grind the following ingredients in a food processor,
and mix well:

    5 cups walnuts
    3 cups raisins
    3 Tablespoons raw carob powder
    1 teaspoon Frontier's butterscotch flavor
    1/4 teaspoon salt
    1 cup dry, hulled buckwheat (optional)

Mix well, and form into a layer of crust. For the
fruit layer, use sweet raw berries such as strawberries, raspberries, blackberries, blueberries, mulber-
ries, gooseberries, etc.

Topping
Blend the following ingredients in a blender until
smooth:

    1/2 cup water
    1 cup raw tahini
    4 Tablespoons honey
    3 Tablespoons raw carob powder
    1 teaspoon vanilla
    1/4 teaspoon salt

It's important to put the water in first because this
prevents the tahini from sticking to the blades of
the blender. Spread the topping evenly over the

crust, or squeeze out through a decorating bag.
Decorate with fruits, berries, and nuts. Chill.

Serves 12

Sergei's Amazing Truffles

1 cup walnuts (don't soak nuts for this recipe)
1/2 cup of your favorite pitted dates
1/4 cup water
4 Tablespoons raw carob
1/4 teaspoon salt

Blend the walnuts and dates in a food processor
till the mixture is smooth. Mix in the raw carob
and water. Shape the mixture into small balls and
roll the balls in carob. Decorate with your favorite
fruit.

Makes 8-12 truffles

Halvah

In a bowl mix the following:
    16 ounces raw tahini
    1 cup of shredded dried coconut
    1/2 cup honey
    1/4 teaspoon salt (optional)
    1/2 cup pistachios (optional)

On a dehydrator tray, make a 2-inch thick cracker.
Dry for 6-8 hours at 100 degrees F. Chill for 1-2
hours in a freezer before serving.

Serves 24

Apple Sauce

    2 cups water
    4 cups chopped apples
    1 cup raisins
    1/4 of a lemon with peel
    1/2 teaspoon cinnamon

Begin to blend. While blending throw in more
apples until desired thickness. Decorate with fresh
berries or raisins.

Serves 6

Alla's Cranberry Scones

Ingredients:
- 2 cups grated apples
- 2 cups carrot pulp from carrot juice
- 2 cups raisins or chopped dates
- 1 cup cranberries, fresh or dry
- 2 Tablespoons honey
- 2 cups almonds, ground
- 1 cup flaxseed blended with 1 cup water
- 1/4 cup olive oil

Mix well. You have to experiment to get the desired consistency. Shape into scones and put on dehydrator sheets. Dehydrate at 105-115 degrees for several hours; approximately 4 hours on one side, and then flip for 3 hours on opposite side.

Makes 24 scones

Banana Ice Cream

4 pealed and frozen bananas

Put ingredients through a Champion Juicer with the blank attachment in place. Sprinkle with nuts, carob powder or ground flaxseed.

Serves 3

Amazing Almonds

9 cups almonds
2 cups Nama Shoyu
5 cups water

Keep the almonds submerged in this solution for eight hours (overnight). Then mix them with the following:

3 Tablespoons garlic powder
5 Tablespoons onion powder
5 Tablespoons lemon juice

Dry until crunchy.   *Serves 5*

Morning Cereal

3 cups raw rolled oats
1 cup water
1 Tablespoon oil
2 Tablespoons honey
1/5 teaspoon salt (optional)

Mix well, and serve with chopped fruit.

Serves 3

Photo Album

The Boutenko Family in 2004.

Victoria (above) and Igor (below) in 1993.

Boutenko family after three months on raw food.

Igor after six months on raw food.

Victoria after six months on raw food.

Boutenko family successfully finished Boulder Boulder
10k race after four months on raw food, May 1993.

Sergei creating a raw feast for friends
after four years on raw food.

Valya enjoying wild malva from
the backyard garden in 1997.

At the trailhead of the Pacific Crest Trail,
on the Mexican border, April 3, 1998.

The wild thistle tastes sweet on the trail.

Rainproof "shoes."

Valya and Victoria by a blue lake.

Teva sandals — the best hiking shoes!

The garbage bags — the best raingear.

Collecting wild edibles for meals along the trail.

Good morning at 7,000 feet.

We built a shelter and lived in it for
three days while it rained.

Victoria at Mt. Laguna.

The Boutenkos finish the Pacific Crest Trail, on the
Canadian border, September 16, 1998.

Victoria at WellSprings Garden Café in 1998.

Sweet dumpling squash stuffed with
the garden burger mixture.

Firebird cake

Un-chocolate cake

Almond cake

Live bread

Real RAWssian borscht

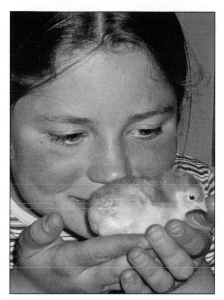

Valya likes her chicken to stay alive.

Sergei's favorite food.

ORDER FORM

Raw Family Publishing
Online orders: www.RawFamily.com
E-mail: Victoria@rawfamily.com
Postal orders: P.O. Box 172, Ashland, OR 97520

Please send me:

(___) copies of *Raw Family* @ $9.95

(___) copies of *Eating Without Heating* @ $11.95

(___) copies of *12 Steps to Raw Food* @ $11.95

(___) copies of videotape *Raw Gourmet Dishes Simplified* @ $19.95

(___) copies of videotape *Is Raw Food For You?* @ $11.95

(___) copies of set of videotapes (3 tapes) *12 Steps to Raw Foods Workshop* @ $59.95

Shipping and handling: $3.00 each book or tape

Payment: Check, credit card or money order

TOTAL: $_____

Name: _____

Address: _____

City: _____ State: _____ Zip: _____

Telephone: _____

E-mail address: _____

Wholesale discounts available on large quantities.